Hands-on Nativity Craft Book

Crafts by Christina Goodings
Photography by John Williams
Illustration by Adrian Barclay

Contents

LION
CHILDREN'S

1 Welcome to Bethlehem

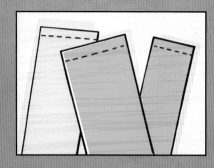

1 Decide on how many buildings you want, and how tall and wide each should be. Each one begins with a rectangle with enough overlap for the roof.

2 Choose the shape of the roof. The buildings here have either half circles or triangles. Measure and cut the roof from card, and glue it on.

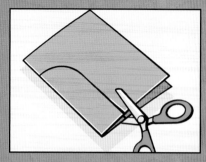

3 Fold a piece of card for the doors. Draw a half arch as shown. Cut out the shape, and cut along the fold. Glue on the doors.

Cut out or punch other shapes for all the details.

The story of the Nativity is the story of Jesus' birth. It is found in the Bible, in the Gospels of Matthew and Luke.

Before Jesus was born, the Roman emperor Augustus decreed that everyone had to go to their home town to register as taxpayers. Joseph lived and worked in Nazareth, but his family were from Bethlehem.

The little hilltop town was already famous as the place where King David had been born.

The Jewish people believed that their next great king would also be born in Bethlehem.

2 Joseph

1 Copy the standing figure support shape at the back of this book onto thin card and cut it out.

2 Next, copy the tunic shape onto thin card, making sure it's slightly larger all around than the support shape. Cut it out.

3 Copy the head and hair onto thick skin-tone paper. Use marker to draw the face and hairstyle. Cut it out.

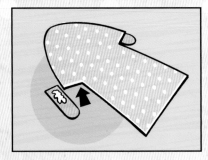

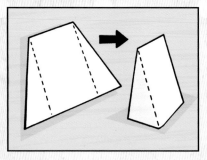

4 Next, copy the tunic shape onto the paper you have chosen. Cut it out, letting it go a little higher at the neck. Cut hands in skin tones and glue these on the back of the sleeves.

5 Now glue the tunic on the support. Add extra cut-outs for a hat, belt, or cloak as you wish, and the head on top last.

6 Cut a piece of card like the one at the back of the book. Fold as shown and glue to the back of your figure so it stands up.

Joseph had been looking forward to making Mary his wife when he heard troubling news: she was expecting a baby, and he wasn't the father.

He knew nothing of Mary's side of the story. The angel Gabriel had come to Nazareth with a message for Mary: that God had chosen her to be the mother of his Son, Jesus – the Christ, the messiah, God's chosen king.

Then, in a dream, an angel spoke to Joseph. God wanted him to marry Mary and take care of her and Jesus.

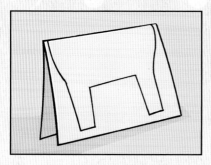
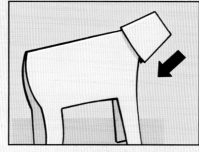

Donkey

1 Make a donkey by cutting the donkey shape at the back of the book onto folded card.

2 Then cut out the neck shape on folded card and glue it to the body.

3 Copy and cut out the head, and add a muzzle. Draw the features. Finally add a tail.

Create your own Nativity characters to the size or style you like. The method used for the character here is easy to adapt for all the Nativity people.

3 The stable

1 Select a cardboard box to the size you need for your Nativity scene, or you could make a box. Paint the stable and leave to dry.

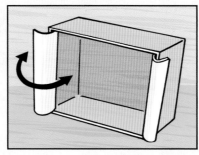

2 Cut rectangles of card to wrap around the sides. Glue in place.

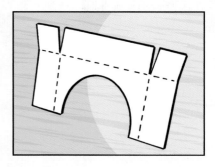

3 Next, rule a rectangle on a piece of card just a little wider than your stable box and the depth you want your arch to be. Add a border to the top and sides to match the depth of your stable.

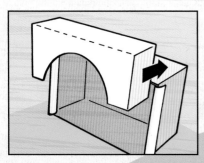

4 Fold the card as shown to make a piece that fits on the top of your stable box.

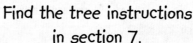

Find the tree instructions in section 7.

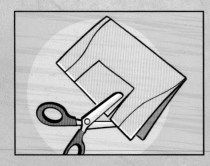

Ox

1 Make an ox for the stable scene by cutting the ox shape at the back of the book onto folded card.

2 Copy and cut out the head and horns. Glue the horns on the back of the head, and glue this on the body. Add a tail and draw the features.

When Mary and Joseph reached Bethlehem, there was no room left at the inn. How could Mary not be upset? Her baby was soon to be born, and she needed a place to shelter.

Joseph and Mary ended up in a stable. In those days, farm animals were often sheltered at one end of a farmhouse. Perhaps, for people who were not wealthy, it did not seem too unusual as a place to stay in an emergency.

4 The baby in the manger

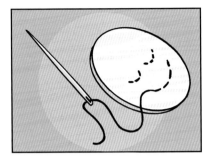

1 First make a swaddled baby. Draw an oval in felt for the face and body and cut it out. Thread a needle with dark yarn and stitch two eyes and a mouth.

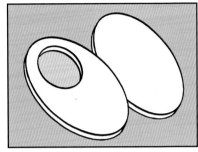

2 Next cut two ovals in white felt, a little larger than the first oval. Cut a circle out of one so the face can show through.

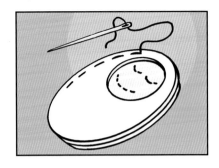

3 Sandwich the face and body piece between the white pieces. Stitch all around.

4 Wrap wool around the finished baby like swaddling bands.

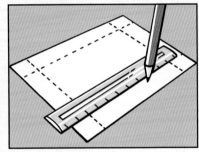

5 Next make a manger for the baby. Begin with a rectangle of card that will hold the baby, then measure and rule a border.

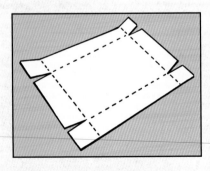

6 Use a rule to crease along the edges as shown, and make snips.

7 Fold up the ends, and then fold in the side tabs at an angle as shown. Glue in place.

Mary and Joseph took shelter in a stable. It was time for Mary's baby to be born: little baby Jesus.

She wrapped him in the traditional way: first a blanket, then strips of cloth to hold it snugly in place. These strips were called swaddling bands.

She had no cradle, but a sturdy feeding trough for the animals made a good substitute. Mary laid her swaddled baby in that manger.

Find these Mary and angel templates at the back of the book.

5 Costumes for boys and girls

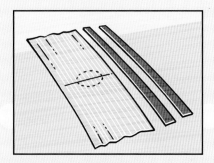

Joseph was a carpenter, an ordinary working man. The shepherds on the hillside who came to the stable to see Jesus were also working men. They are usually depicted in striped tunics that give a similar look to handwoven cloth of the period.

Tunic

Take a long rectangular piece of fabric. Fold in half and cut a hole for the head. If needed cut extra strips of material for the tunic. Drape material over and secure with a belt.

If you wish, cut down the middle of the front of the tunic to make a sleeveless jacket. Add a contrasting tunic and tie with a fabric belt for a rustic look and feel.

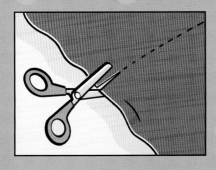
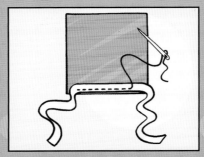
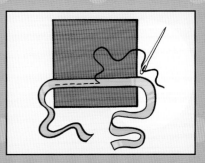

Headdress

1 Cut a square of fabric. Each side should be about the same as the width of the tunic. Finish by turning in a small edge and stitch all around.

2 Stitch a ribbon along one of the edges as shown. To wear, tie ribbon ends under the fabric at the back of the neck.

2 Stitch a contrasting ribbon or band as shown. To wear, arrange like a headband and tie ribbon ends at the back of the head.

You could make a pleat at the centre front of the tunic to hold the fullness compared with the back. Stitch or pin, adding in beads if you wish.

Mary is usually depicted in blue, to remind people of God blessing her with heavenly grace.

The angel Gabriel said to her, when announcing that she was to be the mother of Jesus, "The Lord is with you and has greatly blessed you."

6 Crib scene

Find the star
instructions in
section 9.

In the traditional Nativity scene, shepherds have come to the stable to find the baby Jesus.

The ox and the donkey recall words of the prophet Isaiah – that these animals know who their master is, even though people may not recognize their Lord and God.

A star hangs over the place where Jesus lies, and wise men from the east arrive, each bearing one of the three gifts.

7 The shepherds and their sheep

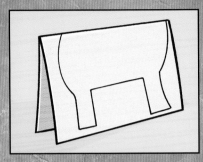

1 Copy the sheep shape at the back of the book onto folded card. Cut out.

2 Copy the head and ear shapes and cut out. Glue the ears onto the back of the head. Add features in marker.

3 Punch flower shapes, or tear irregular bits of white paper, and glue in overlapping rows on the sheep's body. Cut and glue on a tail. Finally, glue on the head.

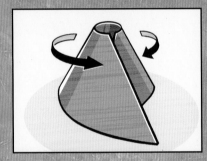

1 Copy the trunk template from the back cover. Cut out on brown card, and curl into a cone. Stick with double-sided tape.

2 Copy the two branch shapes. Cut out in green card, and insert into the cone tree trunk.

3 Thread a bead on wire, then bend in half. Insert into the tree trunk.

If you wish, turn in a tiny amount of each of the legs to make the animal stand better.

On the night that Jesus was born, there were some shepherds out on the hillsides near Bethlehem, guarding their sheep.

Suddenly an angel appeared and told them the good news: God's chosen king had been born in Bethlehem, and was now wrapped in swaddling bands and lying in a manger.

Then a multitude of angels appeared, praising God and singing:

"Glory to God in the highest heaven, and peace on earth to those with whom he is pleased!"

When the angels had gone, the shepherds went to Bethlehem. They found the stable, and the baby.

Shepherds

Make shepherd figures similar to those for Joseph.

8 Angels

Halo

1 Cut a strip of card just long enough to fit around the wearer's head, edge to edge.

2 Glue ribbon on top. Fold in the ends and punch a hole.

3 Cut out heart shapes and glue. Then add stick-on jewels. Thread a satin ribbon through the holes as shown.

Angel

1 Copy the angel template from the back cover. Copy and cut out the halo, wings, and head, and make hand shapes.

2 Stick together as shown.

This is what the angel said to the shepherds: "Don't be afraid! I am here with good news for you, which will bring great joy to all the people. This very day in David's town your Saviour was born – Christ the Lord! And this is what will prove it to you: you will find a baby wrapped in strips of cloth and lying in a manger."

An angel is traditionally shown wearing white with silver and gold. This tunic has a pleat at the neck, stitched with beads.

9 Bright stars

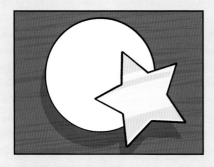
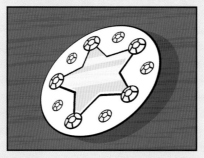

Little stars

1 Cut or punch a circle and a star that fits within it.

2 Glue the star on the circle and add shimmering jewels.

If you wish, add a hanging loop on the back of each star and hang on the tree.

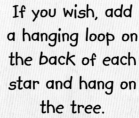

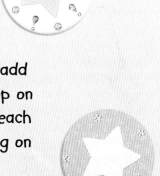

At the time that Jesus was born, wise men in lands to the east saw a new star. They believed it was a sign that a new king had been born to the Jewish people.

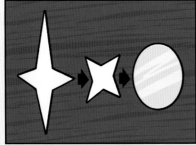

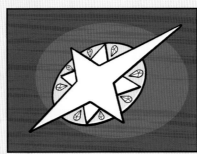

1 Copy the star shapes on the back cover and cut them out in your choice of card. Assemble and glue in this order: circle, small star, big star.

2 Decorate as extravagantly as you like.

3 Cut a rectangle of green paper and curl into a tube. Check it will fit on the top spike of the tree. Then tape the star to this cone and fit on the tree.

10 The wise men

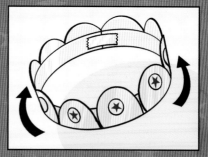

A crown

1 Cut a strip of metallic card to fit around the wearer's head with an overlap. Mark this, but leave flat.

2 Cut circles of the same card, and cut each in half. Glue these around the strip. Then add jewels or stickers to decorate.

3 Finally, curl the strip into a circle, check the fit, and glue or tape in place.

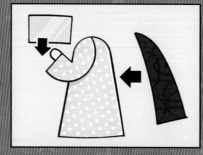

Wise men

1 Copy the wise men head and tunic templates from the back cover.

2 Cut the arm shape. Add a hand, gift, and cloak, and glue them onto the tunic.

3 Draw the face and hair. Glue the head onto the body and add a crown. Glue on the base and stand. Decorate with jewels.

They followed the star to Jerusalem, where King Herod ruled the Jews on behalf of the Roman emperor. Herod's advisors reminded him of an ancient prophecy that one day God's chosen king would be born in Bethlehem.

He sent the wise men there, hoping they would spy out a rival and bring back useful intelligence.

11 Gifts for a king

Square gift

1 Take a square of rich fabric. Place a box on it diagonally to the sides as shown.

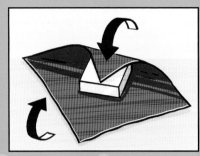

2 Fold first one corner over, then the opposite corner.

3 Take the two remaining corners and tie in a knot. Tie in extra ribbons and decorations if you wish.

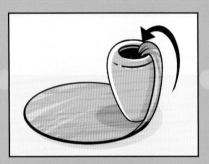

Gift in a pot

1 Place a pot or container in the middle of a large circle of paper. Smooth the paper up the sides and tuck the ends in.

2 Now place the pot on a much larger circle of fabric. Gather the fabric up around the pot and tie with a ribbon.

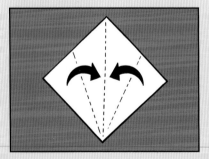

Two-tone gift

1 Take two squares of contrasting paper, each the same size. Lightly rule a diagonal on the wrong side. Now fold in the sides to make a kite shape.

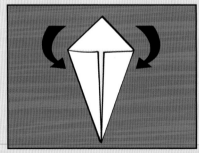

2 Fold the top down as shown by the arrows.

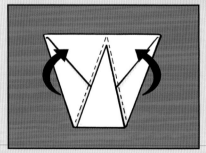

3 Fold the bottom point to the middle of the top side. Then fold the sides in along the lines shown, crease, and unfold.

When the wise men reached the place where Jesus was, they brought out gifts that were fit for a king: gold, frankincense, and myrrh.

In a dream, an angel warned them not to tell Herod that they had found the baby king. Instead, they went home by a different road.

An angel also warned Joseph about Herod's anger, and that Joseph should take Mary and the child to faraway Egypt until Herod died.

Joseph did so at once. He knew it was his duty to keep the child safe, so he could grow up to show the world God's love and blessing.

4 Make the second piece in the same way, but when you get to the end of stage 2, turn the piece over before doing the folds in step 3.

5 Fit the pieces together, tucking the points in the flaps.

6 Close the two halves as shown, tucking the sides of one half in the flaps of the other. Decorate.

Templates

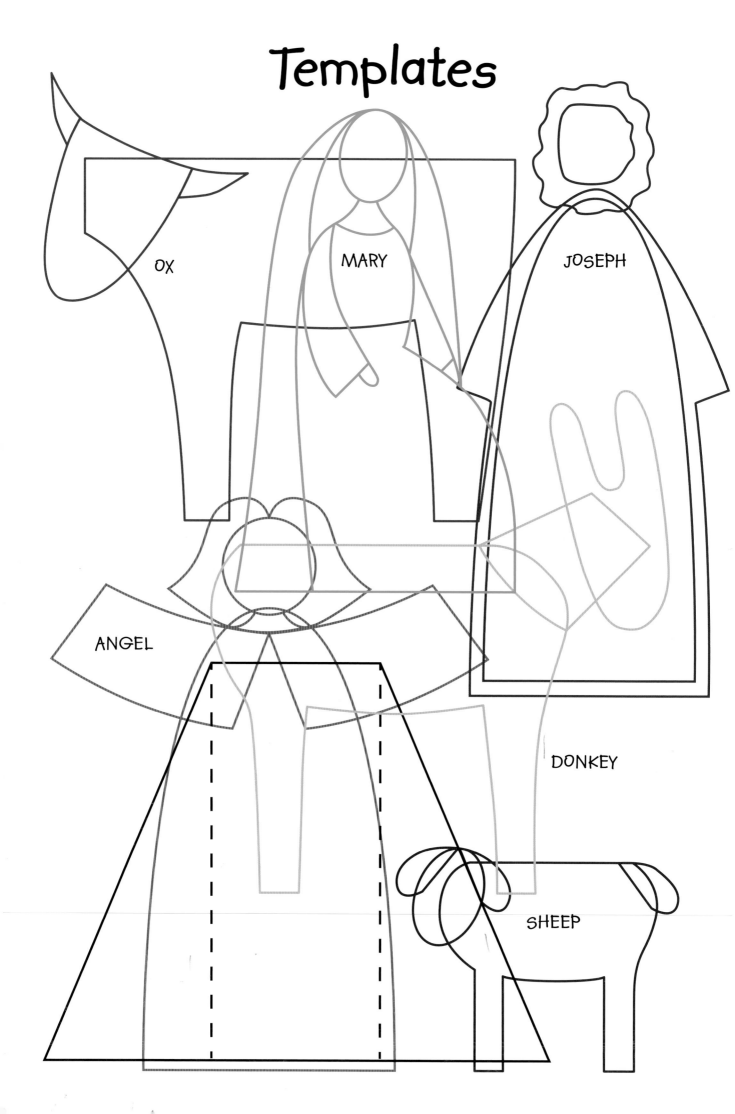

OX

MARY

JOSEPH

ANGEL

DONKEY

SHEEP